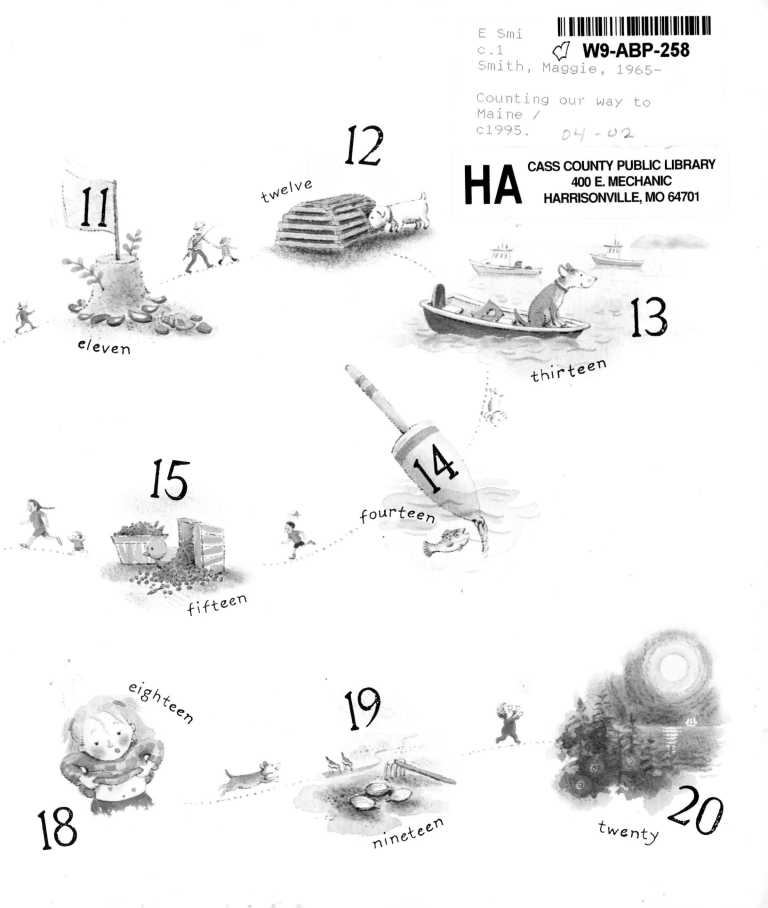

eleven 11

12 *twelve*

13 *thirteen*

15 *fifteen*

14 *fourteen*

eighteen 18

19 *nineteen*

20 *twenty*

Counting Our Way to Maine

A MELANIE KROUPA BOOK

ORCHARD BOOKS
95 Madison Avenue, New York, NY 10016

Manufactured in the United States of America
Printed by Barton Press, Inc.
Bound by Horowitz/Rae
Book design by Sylvia Frezzolini Severance

10 9 8 7 6 5 4 3 2

The text of this book is set in 20 point Goudy.
The illustrations are watercolor, gouache, and pastel with ink and pencil line.

Library of Congress Cataloging-in-Publication Data
Smith, Maggie, date.   Counting our way to Maine / Maggie Smith.   p. cm.
"A Melanie Kroupa book"—Half t.p.
Summary: On a trip to Maine, the family counts from one baby to twenty fireflies.
ISBN 0-531-06884-6. — ISBN 0-531-08734-4 (lib. bdg.)
[1. Voyages and travels—Fiction. 2. Counting.] I. Title.
PZ7.S65474Co 1995   [E]—dc20   94-24874

Maggie Smith
Counting Our Way to Maine

ORCHARD BOOKS   NEW YORK

for Mom & Dad

For our trip to Maine this summer
we packed one baby,

2 two dogs,

3 and three bicycles.

4 As we left the city behind us,
we passed four taxicabs

5 and five smokestacks.

6 We had to stop for the bathroom six times!

7 When we were halfway there, we stopped again and ate seven ice creams.

8 Then we climbed into the car and drove over and around eight mountains.

9 Before long we had to stop again.
Nine deer watched us.

10 When we finally arrived at the cottage, there were ten slugs waiting on the steps!

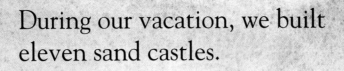

11 During our vacation, we built eleven sand castles.

12

We went down to the dock and saw
twelve lobster pots

13
and thirteen boats.

14

As the fog lifted, we spotted fourteen buoys bobbing on the waves.

15

One hot day we climbed a steep hill and filled fifteen boxes with blueberries.

16 And the next day we made sixteen blueberry pies.

17

We went into the woods early one morning
and found seventeen mushrooms.

18 When we got back to the cottage, we counted eighteen mosquito bites!

19 For our cookout the last night we went to a nearby cove and dug nineteen clams.

20 That evening, as the tide crept in to say good-bye,

we chased twenty fireflies.

The next morning we let our fireflies go.

And for our trip back to the city
we packed one baby . . .

1   one

two   2

3   three

4   four

RESTROOM

6   six

5   five

10   ten

seven   7

9   nine

8   eight

sixteen   16

17   seventeen